D1359630

BULLYING
Bully No More

JUNE HUNT

ROSE PUBLISHING/ASPIRE PRESS

Torrance, California

ROSE PUBLISHING/ASPIRE PRESS

Bullying: Bully No More
Copyright © 2014 Hope For The Heart
All rights reserved.
Aspire Press, a division of Rose Publishing, Inc.
4733 Torrance Blvd., #259
Torrance, California 90503 USA
www.aspirepress.com

Register your book at www.aspirepress.com/register
Get inspiration via email, sign up at www.aspirepress.com

The information and solutions offered in this resource are a result of
years of Bible study, research, and practical life application. They are
intended as guidelines for healthy living and are not a replacement
for professional medical advice. JUNE HUNT and HOPE FOR
THE HEART make no warranties, representations, or guarantees
regarding any particular result or outcome. Any and all express or
implied warranties are disclaimed. Please consult qualified medical,
pastoral, and psychological professionals regarding individual
conditions and needs. JUNE HUNT and HOPE FOR THE HEART
do not advocate that you treat yourself or someone you know and
disclaim any and all liability arising directly or indirectly from the
information in this resource.

For more information on Hope For The Heart, visit
www.hopefortheheart.org or call 1-800-488-HOPE (4673).

Printed in the United States of America
010514RRD

CONTENTS

Dear Friend,

How I wish you could meet my young friend, Jessica. Raised in an affirming home by encouraging parents, she's bright, respectful, hard-working—the kind of teenager who desires to spread *truth* wherever she goes. That's why it didn't surprise me to learn about her reaction to seeing a couple of classmates cheating on a math test.

Honor compelled her to privately tell her teacher about the matter. No, that didn't surprise me at all. But what happened next was a tragedy!

When confronted, the two accused students turned on their teacher, alleging that *she* had trumped up the charges. To gain credibility, the teacher divulged that a *student* had been an eyewitness to the cheating. Later, Jessica's mom, Hannah, a former HOPE FOR THE HEART team member, confided that, by naming Jessica as the source, the teacher "fed my daughter to the wolves."

Indeed, a feeding frenzy ensued. Hannah explained, "The two girls made it their personal mission to terrorize Jessica. They told the teacher and their friends that my daughter was lying. In volleyball, the girls would intentionally spike the ball to hit her head. After being injured during one game, she could no longer play. And these girls stayed on the attack: 'She's just faking it to sabotage the team. After all, we know she is a liar.'"

At first, Jessica did what many bullied children do: she suffered in silence and kept the problem from her parents. She thought that ignoring it would make it go away. Her mom, the school choir director, admitted, "I wish I could say the terror lessened once my husband and I got involved ... but it didn't. This was a torturous time for our entire family." In truth, they each witnessed the impact of Proverbs 29:22 upon their lives, *"An angry person stirs up conflict, and a hot-tempered person commits many sins."*

Hannah added, "Before the year ended, my husband (a coach at the school) changed jobs, and we found a new school for Jessica. I'm happy to say the new school provided a time of healing for all of us. Still, we'll never forget this difficult chapter in our lives—especially the terrible pain that bullies can inflict and the fallout when bullying is mishandled or ignored."

Bullying is usually not a onetime act, but is rather repeated, harmful harassment. Therefore, those who are bullied live with continual fear of future abuse, and some even become bullies to try to stop the barrage of belittling upon themselves. Indeed, most bullies likely have been bullied for a period of time in their past. Proverbs 24:1–2 sums up the inner world of bullies: " ... *their hearts plot violence, and their lips talk about making trouble."*

While Jessica's story has a positive ending, many instances of bullying do not. Bullying can lead to a host of emotional problems, including depression, anxiety attacks, even suicide. This is why early reporting and intervention are crucial.

And this is why I'm grateful you hold this book in your hands! Each page is filled with *biblical hope and practical help* to stop this pervasive and growing problem. Yes, bullying can be curtailed by skillful intervention.

After you read this book, pass it on to others who can benefit from it: parents, youth workers, teachers and other educators. Typically, there are three participants in bullying: the bully, the bullied, and the bystander—and the bystander has the most power!

Realize, your life can make a difference—you can bring life-changing hope to someone's bullied heart.

Yours in the Lord's hope,

June Hunt

P.S. The Bible reminds us, "*The prudent see danger and take refuge, but the simple keep going and pay the penalty*" (Proverbs 22:3).

(Names changed to protect privacy.)

BULLYING
Bully No More

"Stop it! Don't talk to her that way!" "Stop making fun of them! That's mean!" "Stop hitting him! Or I will tell someone *right now*!" If only *bystanders* would speak up when they see belittling behavior. If only they were taught to speak up and speak out, there would be fewer bullies and fewer victims of bullying.

Sometimes recognizing bullying can be a challenge. Fights between friends may be simply that—"friendly fights." But not so with bullies. Bullying takes place when one person possesses more power than another person and intentionally leverages that power to threaten, scare, isolate, or hurt that other person.

Between the three groups—the *bullies*, the *bullied*, and the *bystanders*—those with the most power to cause the most change are the bystanders. Learning the right assertive response can curtail bullying sooner rather than later.

The Bible's book of wisdom describes the type of words that flow from both those who are right and those who are wrong toward others, from those who help and from those who hurt ...

"The mouth of the righteous is a fountain of life, but the mouth of the wicked conceals violence."
(Proverbs 10:11)

DEFINITIONS

Phoebe Prince was the "new girl" who caused quite a stir—a 15-year-old who arrived from Ireland with her mother in the fall of 2009.

Being in a new country and a new school, Phoebe was excited and optimistic about her future. She even signed off her text messages, "Life is an opportunity in itself."[1]

But by January 14, 2010, Phoebe believed there was only one option available to her, only one path to peace. She saw only one way to escape the constant criticism, the relentless barrage of *bullying*.

The Bible describes such desperate despair ...

> "What I feared has come upon me;
> what I dreaded has happened to me.
> I have no peace, no quietness;
> I have no rest, but only turmoil."
> (Job 3:25–26)

Somehow Phoebe ignited a fuse of jealousy—a fuse that caused a firestorm that blazed out of control. Some said it was jealousy over her looks—her raven hair and sparkling eyes—that inflamed a band of popular girls at South Hadley High School in Massachusetts. Others said it was jealousy over boys—the two guys she dated—that provoked a warning from a notorious clique that fits the profile of the proverbial "Mean Girls." They stalked the hallways projecting their prominence and power, and they issued a directive to Phoebe: Stay away from "people's men."[2]

Phoebe had previously caught the eye of Sean, the captain of the football team, who began dating her but failed to mention he already had a girlfriend. When Phoebe found out about Kayla, she apologized to her and assumed all was resolved.

The Irish teen later dated Austin, which raised the ire of his on-again, off-again girlfriend—the not-so-nice Flannery. This dating dilemma prompted Phoebe to offer yet another apology. But Phoebe's pursuit of peace was met only with threats—threats of violence, which is characteristic of bullying.[3]

The arrogant heart of a bully is described in Scripture—one who hunts down victims ...

"In his arrogance the wicked man hunts down the weak, who are caught in the schemes he devises."
(Psalm 10:2)

The "art" of bullying casts a wide net:[4]

▶ **Bullying** is any deliberate, hostile, physical, psychological, or verbal activity involving an imbalance of power with the intent to harm and induce fear.

▶ **Bullying** seeks to emotionally harass or physically harm others, even to the extent of damaging property and destroying pets, in order to cause debilitating fear and distress.

▶ **Bullying** is persistent, pervasive abuse that creates an intimidating or terrorizing environment.

▶ **Bullying** is not a onetime act, but rather repeated, persistent harassment by a person or group, often targeting someone perceived to be weaker physically or psychologically.

▶ **Bullying** does not stop without intervention, but it must stop!

The following acrostic addresses the four primary components found in bullying:

S—**Severe**: Intensely harsh, stern, and critical

T—**Threatening:** Intentionally fear-producing and terrorizing

O—**Out-of-Balance:** Imbalance of power; ill-matched and unequal strength

P—**Persistent**: Incessant, continual, not a onetime act

These words of Scripture will apply to bullies ....

> "Because of your stubbornness
> and your unrepentant heart,
> you are storing up wrath against yourself
> for the day of God's wrath,
> when his righteous judgment
> will be revealed."
> (Romans 2:5)

Relationally Aggressive Bullies

QUESTION: "What is Relational Aggression?"

ANSWER: *Relational Aggression* (RA) is a type of bullying practiced especially by girls and is designed to intimidate, control, or hurt a victim's social relationships and reputation by forming manipulative relationships.[5] Their indirect acts and attacks can appear like a "love/hate" relationship that can include making another girl look foolish, stealing her friends, and telling others not to associate with her.

Relationally aggressive bullies lure victims closer and closer, pretending to be friends—even "best friends"—only to deal the devastating blow of total rejection, betrayal, and abandonment.

In the Bible, David describes this kind of betrayal ...

> "They repay me evil for good,
> and hatred for my friendship."
> (Psalm 109:5)

Phoebe was a victim of viciousness that depleted her vitality. The extreme bullying at school and cyberbullying online obliterated her optimism, filled her with fear, and weakened her will.

According to a friend in Ireland, Phoebe's initial coping strategy was to "keep her head high, smile and just let it go past her."[6]

However, Phoebe just couldn't shake the taunts, verbal assaults, and painful postings on a social media site from the "Mean Girls" who told her, "Go kill yourself."[7]

How hauntingly true-to-life is the following Psalm ...

> "The enemy pursues me ... crushes me
> to the ground ... makes me dwell in the
> darkness like those long dead.
> So my spirit grows faint within me;
> my heart within me is dismayed."
> (Psalm 143:3–4)

Conflict exists in every relationship. But there are clear and distinct differences between conflicts in healthy relationships and those in bullying relationships.

HEALTHY COMMON CONFLICTS	UNHEALTHY BULLYING CONFLICTS
Involve equal power between people	Involve unequal power between the bully and the bullied
Occur occasionally	Occur repeatedly
Often unintentional	Always intentional
Seldom serious	Often serious
Not power-seeking	Always power-seeking
Usually result in remorse	Never result in remorse
Occur with the desire to solve the problem	Occur with no desire to solve the problem
Never initiated to cause harm	Always initiated to cause harm

The Word of God gives this eye-opening description of the relationship between a bully and conflict ...

"A troublemaker and a villain, who goes
about with a corrupt mouth,
who winks maliciously with his eye, signals
with his feet and motions with his fingers,
who plots evil with deceit in his heart—
he always stirs up conflict."
(Proverbs 6:12–14)

BULLYING CAN'T BE RESOLVED BY CONVENTIONAL MEANS.[8]

- Bullying involves an ongoing abusive relationship of unequal power, producing an abusive cycle that children and teens are not normally equipped to resolve.

  - Traditional conflict resolution is designed to address common conflicts in which power is roughly equal.
  - Using traditional methods to resolve bullying could subject the bullied child to further victimization.

- Mediation and traditional counseling generally find some portion of fault with each party.

  - In a bullying situation, all blame must be assigned to the bully.
  - A bullied child should not be asked nor expected to accept responsibility for the abuse.

- Most mediators are trained to avoid taking a moral position on the issues they confront.

  - It's crucial for involved adults to articulate the wrongness of bullying.
  - It's equally crucial for bullies to accept responsibility for their wrong actions and for those who have been victimized to understand they are not at fault.

▶ Traditional abuse programs may assign too much responsibility for the students to resolve.

- Bullying involves complex behavioral dynamics that are tricky even for trained adults to handle.
- Relying on traditional conflict resolution methods may lead adults to conclude wrongly that their involvement is not necessary.
- Students are not equipped to handle harassment and abuse alone. A support network of parents, school officials, and peers is necessary to overcome an established bullying culture.

Therefore seek counsel from those who have expertise in effectively working with bullies.

"The heart of the discerning
acquires knowledge,
for the ears of the wise seek it out."
(Proverbs 18:15)

Phoebe was outnumbered and overpowered, surrounded by bullies determined to push her to the brink.

On January 14, 2010, Phoebe was in the school library when a deeply troubling incident took place. Joining her tormentors was one of her very first friends, Sean—one of the young men she dated. Obscenities spewed in her direction, then Phoebe's bullies wrote them on the library sign-in sheet.[9]

Once hopeful, now horrified, Phoebe lamented in a text message, "I can't take much more."[10] By the following afternoon, she determined she wouldn't take any more. As Phoebe walked home from school, one of the "Mean Girls" chucked an empty can at her, sealing the dark decision preoccupying her mind. She arrived home picked up a scarf (the new Christmas gift from her sister), slipped it around her neck, and, in the stairwell of their new home, she hung herself. She ended her torment by ending her life![11]

Phoebe Prince would never again feel the pain of bullying, but that didn't end the bullying. Following Phoebe's death, the "Mean Girls" logged onto their computers and mocked her death.[12]

The Sequence

Ultimately, bullying involves a process of depersonalization and desensitization enabling both the bullies and many bystanders to commit more and more severe acts of violence against those being targeted for bullying.[13]

▶ **The bully** evaluates the environment, locates a victim, then checks out the crowd of bystanders.

▶ **The bully** makes degrading remarks to the victim then waits for a response from the victim and bystanders.

▶ **The target** either responds with strength (forceful disapproval) or with weakness (fearful uneasiness).

▶ **The bully** will respond in a variety of ways:

- *Leader bullies* begin the bullying and then try to coax followers to join them.

- *Follower bullies* or "*henchmen*" don't start the bullying but enjoy taking an active role.

- *Passive bullies* or *supporters* openly endorse the bullying by laughing at or pointing out the victims being bullied but do not take a more active part in bullying.

▶ **The bystanders** can also respond differently:

- *Apathetic bystanders* don't support or become actively involved in the bullying, but neither do they take a stand against it. They believe the bullying is none of their business.

- *Passive bystanders* don't like the bullying and don't want it to continue, but do nothing to stop it.
- *Protective bystanders* are defenders who dislike the bullying and take steps to try to stop it.

▶ **The bully** either escalates the physical or verbal attack and encourages others to join in, or walks off depending on the actions of the bystanders and the one bullied.

▶ **The target** sometimes responds in weakness by engaging in self-bullying and rationalization. ("Yes, I really am stupid." "It's all my fault anyway!")

▶ **The bystander**s who are passive or disengaged either move away out of fear and guilt or join in the bullying.

▶ **The bully** finds new avenues for taunting and tormenting the bullied, becoming more aggressive and instilling more terror.

▶ **The target** spends more and more time trying to find ways to avoid or appease the bully.

▶ **The bully** becomes more vicious and derives increased pleasure from inflicting pain and terror.

▶ **The target** sinks deeper into depression, shame, or rage, dwelling on thoughts of revenge or suicide.

▶ **The bystanders** (disengaged and passive) either blame the victim, bully the victim, feel helpless about the victim, or feel no need to intervene or rescue the victim.

▶ **The bully** continues the succession cycle of violence, often ending up in prison.

▶ **The target** can release pent-up rage in one or more acts of violent aggression, even resulting in the deaths of others or self.

▶ **The bystanders** who are unhelpful live their lives either guilt-ridden or desensitized to accept violence—possibly becoming conduits of violence in their own children's lives.

Scripture gives this warning ...

"There is a way that appears to be right,
but in the end it leads to death."
(Proverbs 14:12)

WHAT IS God's Heart on Bullying?

The tragic death of Phoebe Prince has heightened awareness concerning the viciousness of bullying, especially among vulnerable young people who look to peers to determine their worth and significance. Her death also serves as a sober reminder of the irreversible "finality" of suicide—the unchangeable, needless loss of life. Phoebe's mother shares these poignant words: "There is a dead weight that now sits permanently in my chest."[14]

The Lord is not indifferent about the agony of abuse, for indeed, He knows *there is no excuse for abuse!* Therefore, the Bible states in the strongest terms, *"No one who practices deceit will dwell in my house; no one who speaks falsely will stand in my presence"* (Psalm 101:7).

God's Heart on Bullying

If you struggle with bullying others, remember ...

▶ *God loves you* but hates your evil attitudes and actions. *"To fear the LORD is to hate evil; I hate pride and arrogance, evil behavior and perverse speech"* (Proverbs 8:13).

▶ *God judges you* and will extract payment from you for your hurtful actions. *"Do not be deceived: God cannot be mocked. A man reaps what he sows"* (Galatians 6:7).

▶ *God calls you* to stop bullying once and for all. *"Come back to your senses as you ought, and stop sinning"* (1 Corinthians 15:34).

▶ *God yearns for you* to have a repentant heart and to seek forgiveness so that He might extend mercy and forgiveness to you. *"Have mercy on me, O God, according to your unfailing love; according to your great compassion blot out my transgressions"* (Psalm 51:1).

▶ *God longs for you* to have a heart of compassion for the weak, the oppressed, the bullied. *"Defend the weak and the fatherless; uphold the cause of the poor and the oppressed"* (Psalm 82:3).

If you struggle with being bullied, remember ...

▶ *God sees* your abuse and victimization. *"For there is nothing hidden that will not be disclosed, and nothing concealed that will not be known or brought out into the open"* (Luke 8:17).

▶ *God records* the impact of your mistreatment the tears you have shed. *"Record my misery; list my tears on your scroll—are they not in your record?"* (Psalm 56:8).

▶ *God longs* for you to turn to Him in prayer for strength and protection. *"God is our refuge and strength, an ever-present help in trouble"* (Psalm 46:1).

▶ *God avenges* the helpless, and He will avenge you in His time and in His way as you walk in forgiveness. *"Do not take revenge, my dear friends, but leave room for God's wrath, for it is written: 'It is mine to avenge; I will repay,' says the Lord"* (Romans 12:19). *"On the contrary, repay evil with blessing, because to this you were called so that you may inherit a blessing"* (1 Peter 3:9).

▶ *God will use* your bullying experiences to help and encourage others.

"Praise be to the God and Father of our Lord Jesus Christ, the Father of compassion and the God of all comfort, who comforts us in all our troubles, so that we can comfort those in any trouble with the comfort we ourselves receive from God." (2 Corinthians 1:3–4)

CHARACTERISTICS

Today, Lynzee Benoit is completely "comfortable in her own skin"—but not because others have made her feel so.[15] No, this college graduate has had to process immense pain in order to reach the point where she can truly value being a unique creation of God.

She doesn't spend time comparing her hair, eyes, and makeup to the media's standard of beauty. But Lynzee's journey to her present place of contentment is marked with multiple bouts of embarrassment.

As a fifth grader, she was taunted in a new town, harassed in a new school, and bullied by a boy who continually called her "roadkill." Imagine the impact of such a callous comparison! (Today she still hates that detestable word—*roadkill*.)

Scripture describes just how cruel words can be— especially those that stab the heart ...

> "The words of the reckless
> pierce like swords."
> (Proverbs 12:18)

Born with a cranial midline anomaly affecting her brain, optic nerve, and pituitary gland, Lynzee has been hospitalized more than a dozen times. She has endured four "life or death" brain surgeries to treat hydrocephalus (water on the brain).

Adding to Lynzee's physical struggle is an apparent weakness on the left side of her face that causes a slight drooping. Because she is missing facial and eye muscles, her face appears asymmetrical or slightly slanted, and her eyes don't move in sync. Thus, her appearance draws three types of people: the caring, the curious, and the *cruel*!

In grade school, Lynzee fell prey to those who felt the need to dominate—those who felt superior by making her feel inferior. In addition to the physical pain, her sarcastic classmates pierced her heart and caused overpowering emotional pain.

Tragically, angry bullies cause continual conflict and feel a perverted satisfaction in tormenting victims like Lynzee.

> "An angry person stirs up conflict,
> and a hot-tempered person
> commits many sins."
> (Proverbs 29:22)

The Bully Trait Checklist

Instead of being tender, bullies taunt their victims. To feel superior, they try to make others feel inferior. The four categories of bully traits that follow can help identify those who *bully others* (check all that apply personally or apply to someone you know):[16]

Mental traits of bullies:

☐ Think their behavior is justified and can be quite convincing

☐ Think impulsive thoughts that result in impulsive behaviors

☐ Think it's okay to say mean things ("Your clothes are ugly")

☐ Think that nurturing relationships is a waste of time

☐ Believe they should always be the center of attention

☐ Believe it's okay to be mean because their victims "deserve it"

☐ Believe they are more important than others and exude arrogance

☐ Believe others "owe them" and should be subservient to them

Emotional traits of bullies:

☐ Feel angry when accused of wrongdoing

☐ Feel the need to control and dominate others

☐ Feel no empathy or compassion for others

☐ Feel entitled to get their own way

☐ Feel the need to be first or always win

☐ Feel little or no guilt over their wrongs

- ☐ Feel powerful and exude confidence
- ☐ Feel vengeful when challenged

Behavioral traits of bullies:

- ☐ Act innocent or unaware of their hurtful actions
- ☐ Blame others for their own bad behavior
- ☐ Doodle or draw disturbing images
- ☐ Drawn to websites that promote violence, supremacy, or aggression
- ☐ Exhibit aggressive attitudes that lead to aggressive actions
- ☐ Frequently use alcohol, tobacco, and other drugs
- ☐ Possess strong personalities and charisma
- ☐ Use their verbal skills to persuade peers to do their bidding

Social traits of bullies:

- ☐ Always have to be the center of attention
- ☐ Associate primarily with those who exhibit aggressive behavior
- ☐ Become less popular at the secondary school level
- ☐ Form exclusive friendships or groups
- ☐ Have a reputation for bragging, and being demanding and bossy
- ☐ Initiate harassing phone calls, e-mails, texts, and other means of social media messages
- ☐ Often become ringleaders supported by an entourage of others
- ☐ Wear clothes or hats affiliated with gangs or cliques

One week after Lynzee's birth, the neurologist warned her parents that she may never walk or talk. An early diagnosis of hydrocephalus at nine months of age only added to the physical and mental challenges that lay ahead.

But by the grace of God, the support of her parents, and her own personal perseverance, she courageously overcame most of these challenges. Not only can Lynzee walk and talk, but she is an accomplished and charming, independent young lady.

Although she faced medical obstacles, Lynzee found herself engaged in even more battles. Over time, she endured various forms of verbal, emotional, and physical abuse by those who targeted her with terrorizing tactics.

How accurately the words of Scripture portray her experience ...

> "Terrors startle him on every side
> and dog his every step.
> Calamity is hungry for him;
> disaster is ready for him when he falls."
> (Job 18:11–12)

Bullying can be direct or indirect, overt or covert. Whatever the type, the taunting is always destructive and demoralizing.

Types of Bullying

Bullies target their victims in multiple ways (check all that apply):

Physical bullying:

☐ Pushing, grabbing

☐ Excessive tickling and touching

☐ Punching, poking

☐ Scratching, pinching

☐ Kicking, tripping

☐ Finger bending or breaking

☐ Slapping, hitting

☐ Brandishing a weapon

☐ Biting, spitting

☐ Burning, poisoning

☐ Stealing, breaking possessions

☐ Strangling, suffocating

☐ Hurting or killing pets

☐ Stabbing, shooting

Verbal bullying:

☐ Name-calling, humiliating

☐ Gossiping, spreading rumors

☐ Taunting, teasing

☐ Defaming or degrading graffiti

☐ Insulting, undermining

☐ Ostracizing, isolating

☐ Bad-mouthing, belittling

☐ Threatening, terrorizing

Emotional bullying:

- ☐ Eye rolling, ignoring
- ☐ Excluding, isolating
- ☐ Staring, leering
- ☐ Rejecting, abandoning
- ☐ Withdrawing, finger-pointing
- ☐ Pressuring, coercing
- ☐ Betraying, breaking promises
- ☐ Extorting, blackmailing

Sexual bullying:

- ☐ Sexually taunting, provoking
- ☐ Sexually harassing, tormenting
- ☐ Sexually gesturing, lewdness
- ☐ Sexually grabbing, groping
- ☐ Sexually teasing, seducing
- ☐ Sexually touching, molesting
- ☐ Sexually slandering, gossiping
- ☐ Sexually assaulting, raping

Those who become bullies learn to taunt and torment their victims using multiple methods. As a result those who are bullied feel discouraged and disgraced, reproached and reviled.

"I live in disgrace all day long, and my face is covered in shame at the taunts of those who reproach and revile me because of the enemy, who is bent on revenge."
(Psalm 44:15–16)

WHAT ARE Gender Differences among Bullies?

Lynzee's sense of self-worth spiraled downward as assaults came from both *boys* and *girls*—in different ways and from different directions. In middle school, a boy threw rocks at her during P.E. class. Another boy bashed her head with a book from behind while she was at her locker. Girls gawked rudely at her at the mall, grocery store, and even while on vacation.

Lynzee's emotional stress prompted her mother to find a "code phrase" for them to use when Lynzee was overwhelmed by the stares and jeers of others. This idea came from a favorite children's character, Curious George—a monkey. Her mother tenderly explained to Lynzee, "George is simply curious about everything, just like the people who stare at you." So when Lynzee said, "Mom, I've got some monkey business happening over here," this meant she felt troubled and she needed prayer, and perhaps even a change of environment.

Meanwhile, the psalmist provided comforting counsel for Lynzee, which she took to heart ...

"LORD my God, I take refuge in you; save and deliver me from all who pursue me."
(Psalm 7:1)

Bullying is sometimes tolerated due to outdated cultural ideas about gender roles, such as "boys will be boys." Standards of mutual respect are often eroded by a lack of respect modeled in the home. Some differences exist between boy and girl bullies:

BOY BULLIES	GIRL BULLIES
Known as "Bully Gangsters," Thugs, Hoods, Punks, Goons	Known as "Bully Princesses," Queen Bees, Mean Girls
Target victims one to two years younger	Target same-aged peers
Target both boys and girls	Tend to target only girls
Target students from other grades	Tend to target girls from their own grade
More direct	More manipulative
More likely to inflict physical pain	More likely to inflict emotional pain
More often react with anger and lash out aggressively	More often become depressed, with anger turned inward
More physically aggressive	More malicious with gossip
Threaten physical harm ("If you don't _____, I'll bust your head wide open!")	Threaten ("I won't be your best friend if you _____")

The progression of bullying in Lynzee's life reached a painful climax during her senior year of high school. The abuse took on a more subtle form, but was nonetheless heartrending and brought heaviness to her spirit. Lynzee became a victim of "the silent treatment." She was ignored and socially isolated, sending her the message that *she simply doesn't matter.*

The most popular girl in her senior class of less than 30 students continually maneuvered her head and body around Lynzee to engage others, as if Lynzee didn't even exist.

In the end, coldness proves to be just as cruel as inflammatory words, violating the call of Scripture: *"Dear friends, let us love one another, for love comes from God. Everyone who loves has been born of God and knows God. Whoever does not love does not know God, because God is love"* (1 John 4:7–8).

In God's time, He will lift His hand against all who bully others: *"They will shudder with fear at the uplifted hand that the Lord Almighty raises against them"* (Isaiah 19:16).

Rarely does a child rush in from school and announce, "I got beat up by a bully today!" In fact, many children won't say anything at all. More often, they worry, feel ashamed, or believe that being bullied is their fault. Sadly this shame and self-blame sometimes lasts a lifetime.

Signs of Bullying

The following list indicates those who are *being bullied* (check all that apply):[17]

Mental

☐ Assume, "I'm too weak and unimportant."

☐ Think, "No one understands me."

☐ Presume, "No one will help me."

☐ Decide, "I can't tell others."

☐ Reason, "I can't do anything right."

☐ Believe, "There's no way out."

☐ Consider, "The situation is hopeless."

☐ Determine, "Suicide is my only option."

Emotional

☐ Struggle with poor self-worth

☐ Tend to be sensitive

☐ Become deeply depressed

☐ Feel isolated and lonely

☐ Dread being around people

☐ Worry about facing the future

☐ Fear being easily hurt—again

☐ Hate feeling weak and allowing bullying

Behavioral

☐ Feel controlled by strong, uncaring parent

☐ Negative change in eating patterns

☐ Develop sleep disorders

☐ Suffer from headaches and stomachaches

- ☐ Develop copycat behaviors toward others
- ☐ Keep quiet and do not tell anyone
- ☐ Allow others to control them
- ☐ Hide unexplained bruises and injuries

Social

- ☐ Avoid popular peer-gathering places
- ☐ Withdraw from social activities
- ☐ Receive threatening e-mails and social media messages
- ☐ Get hang-up phone calls
- ☐ Make frequent excuses to miss school
- ☐ Tend to be quiet and introverted
- ☐ Move away from intimacy
- ☐ Retreat from normally enjoyed activities

While these signs may not prove to be related to bullying, these behaviors are worth attention and further investigation.

The Bible says ...

"Let us discern for ourselves what is right;
let us learn together what is good."
(Job 34:4)

Lynzee can be described as an *atypical* victim because of her physical challenges, but she is also a capable victim. She is talented and eager to succeed in life.

Even though she was abused by bullies, Lynzee is a young woman who stays engaged in life and relies on God to be her Strength and Helper. Furthermore, by being a victim of bullying, she has developed a sensitivity toward those who are maligned and mistreated, a tenderness toward those who are discouraged and disadvantaged.

Lynzee's heart reflects God's heart ...

> "You have been a refuge for the poor,
> a refuge for the needy in their distress,
> a shelter from the storm and a shade from
> the heat. For the breath of the ruthless is
> like a storm driving against a wall."
> (Isaiah 25:4)

Bullied victims live with continual fear and expectation of future abuse, or they may become bullies to stop from being bullied. Most bullies have, themselves, been bullied at some point in their past.

The Five Types of Victims

1 **Dependent victims** are members of "enmeshed" families where there is an overdependence on parental support, leaving them socially inept, insecure, and disadvantaged around peers.

2 **Passive victims** are sensitive loners who "don't fit in," lack self-defense skills, don't think quickly on their feet, and have few friends.

3 **Impulsive victims** are easily agitated. They annoy, tease, or taunt bullies, therefore making themselves targets but then are unable to defend themselves.

4 **Capable victims** are talented, bright, and popular. They are good workers who speak up and try to please authority figures by helping or doing extra assignments.

5 **Atypical victims** are different from most other people due to a physical, psychological, or mental anomaly that may diminish their ability to defend themselves.

While the bully seeks to victimize the weak, the Lord instructs us to rescue the weak ...

"Rescue the weak and the needy;
deliver them from the hand of the wicked."
(Psalm 82:4)

As a college student, one day Lynzee was busy at work in a retail store when she became distracted by fingers pointing her way, and then laughing. Two little boys kept staring at her, oblivious to the pain their insensitive behavior was inflicting. Lynzee was distressed and quickly lifted up a prayer, "Lord, Lord, what do I do?" She immediately sensed His response: "Confront them." Lynzee approached the boys, gazed into their eyes, and declared, "This is the way that I was born. This is the way God made me." She turned the focus on her Creator, conveying that what God creates has purpose and significance.

A middle-aged woman approached, identifying herself as the boys' grandmother. Lynzee shared her burdened heart and the woman committed to helping build sensitivity into the boys' spirits. What perfect timing for these two boys. Like Lynzee, the grandmother of the two boys had a vested interest in staving off bullies—she was a special education teacher. Lynzee was grateful for her support, for her willingness to build into these boys' lives the priceless value of every person whom God has created—no matter how He put them together or how they may appear.

God continues to use Lynzee in many ways: to teach, support, encourage, and comfort others. No longer a victim, she refuses to allow the bullying she endured to define who she is or determine her value.

Types & Traits of Bystanders

Consider the following list and check all that apply:

Traits of Apathetic Bystanders:

☐ They feel no obligation to report bullying.

☐ They feel emotionally numb about helping the victims.

☐ They steer clear of situations where bullying may occur.

☐ They don't want to become involved in bullying in any way.

☐ They refuse to take any responsibility to stamp out bullying.

☐ They turn a blind eye and a deaf ear to any talk of bullying.

Traits of Passive Bystanders:

☐ They fear revenge if they report a bullying incident.

☐ They feel a loss of personal safety and self-control.

☐ They withdraw from being a friend of victims for fear of becoming the bully's new target.

☐ They passively accept bullying by not interfering.

☐ They support bullying by laughing and mocking victims.

☐ They sometimes begin to bully others.

Traits of Protective Bystanders:

☐ They stand up to the bully as soon as bullying begins.

☐ They immediately report any and all abuse.

☐ They take a stand against the bully by defending the victim.

☐ They encourage other bystanders to take a stand.

☐ They watch out to protect those who could be targeted by bullies.

☐ They look for ways to get involved in bully prevention campaigns.

Bullies are often hot-tempered and angry. God is clear in His instructions regarding the dangers of associating with those who exhibit such characteristics.

Bystanders who either befriend bullies or consider it none of their business would be wise to heed the instructions of these words from Scripture ...

"Do not make friends
with a hot-tempered person,
do not associate with one easily angered,
or you may learn their ways
and get yourself ensnared."
(Proverbs 22:24–25)

CAUSES

Victoria, the second oldest town in Texas, is filled with history, cattle, and cypress trees that line the banks of the Guadalupe River. It is also known as the "Crossroads of the Coastal Bend" because of its proximity to several major cities.

However, Dr. Steve Hunter identifies Victoria another way: "The very definition of hell. Just the thought of the place still creates terror in the deepest part of my soul. Even now ... when I hear the name, I get the same nauseous feelings down in the deepest pit of my stomach."[18]

Every generation has its bullies who prey mercilessly on those who can't protect themselves. Steve is one who fell victim to their relentless attacks and, even now as a strong adult male, he continues to carry deep scars.

In fact, Steve could have written words much like these ...

" ... people who are wicked and deceitful have opened their mouths against me; they have spoken against me with lying tongues. With words of hatred they surround me; they attack me without cause."
(Psalm 109:2–3)

For Steve, being gifted felt like a curse. Because of accelerated academic performance, Steve was promoted from the third grade to the fifth grade, a leap that became painfully conspicuous by the time he reached the eighth grade. Those around him experienced the changes of puberty, but he remained the same—small in stature and, in comparison, physically underdeveloped.

Warped thoughts of Steve's bullies, and even Steve himself, fueled physical and emotional trauma for more than two years, causing Steve severe mental anguish.

Bullies don't emerge out of a vacuum. Typically, abuse develops from an abusive foundation—an abusive environment or an abusive family. Bullying is what they live, so they learn to be bullied, and to bully. Because they feel angry and bad about themselves, they, in turn, bully younger siblings or find someone weaker to bully.

While people have no say in choosing family, Scripture addresses the importance of choosing friends wisely ...

"The righteous choose
their friends carefully,
but the way of the wicked
leads them astray."
(Proverbs 12:26)

One of the most obvious reasons people bully others is because it works! It gets them what they think they want and need, whether it be a sense of power, position, or possessions.

▶ **Bullies** believe relationships are built on being *the strongest*, because that is true in their families.

▶ **Bullies** are motivated by fear, insecurity, or inferiority in an area of their own lives.

▶ **Bullies** go through life feeling angry and scared, determined that force is the way to deal with their frustrations.

▶ **Bullying** provides a way to feel *in control*.

▶ **Bullies** exclude people, exercise power, and exert control in order to counter fear.

▶ **Bullies** think the antidote to feeling powerless is to feel powerful and that the feeling of power is gained by running roughshod over those who are weaker.

▶ **Bullies** believe that targeting someone they find irritating or "weird" is justified.[19]

▶ **Bullies** lack empathy for victims, identifying bullying as simply a harmless rite of passage. Thus any intervention from bystanders is discouraged.

▶ **Bullies** believe they can bully anyone, anytime, and anywhere ... and get away with it—especially when bystanders fail to stop the bullying.

▶ **Bullies** are encouraged to be aggressive by peers who then respond to them in a more respectful manner.

Often, a bully is two-faced, fooling teachers and parents with positive behavior, while their actions toward peers is cruel and abusive ...

"His talk is smooth as butter, yet war is in his heart; his words are more soothing than oil, yet they are drawn swords."
(Psalm 55:21)

WHAT ARE the Top 10 Fallacies vs. Facts?

Beliefs form the springboard for behavior. If bullies and those they bully hope to change, they need to identify lies and replace them with truths, expose fallacies and correct them with facts. The same is true for those who seek to identify and eradicate bullying.

▶ **THE TOP 10 FALLACIES about Bullying**[20]

- Bullying is normal—simply a rite of passage.
- Bullying doesn't do any real harm.
- Bullying is blatant.
- Bullying is quickly stopped because it draws so much attention.
- Bullying is a rare occurrence.
- Bullies are underachievers with low self-worth.
- Bullies are noticeable and easily recognized.

- Bullies aren't popular or highly regarded by others.
- Bullies eventually mature and grow out of bullying behavior.
- Bullies will always be bullies and victims will always be victims.

▶ THE TOP 10 FACTS about Bullying

- Bullying is inexcusable and can never be dismissed as just "kids being kids."
- Bullying causes great emotional and psychological pain.
- Bullying is subtle and sinister—it mostly happens out of the sight of adults, in school hallways, cafeterias, bathrooms, and on school buses.
- Bullying often goes undetected because victims feel too much shame and embarrassment to report it, feeling it is an indictment of their own inadequacies.
- Bullying is experienced by more than 1 in 5 school children—over 8% of all children report being bullied frequently.[21]
- Bullies carefully hone their arsenals of attack and deliberately develop their destructive demeanor. They gain notice through notoriety and often think they are superior to others.
- Bullies appear "normal" and can hide behind a mask of friendship.

- Bullies perceive and project popularity through power.
- Bullying often leads to criminal behavior: Nearly 60% of boys identified as bullies in grades 6 through 9 were convicted of at least one crime by the age of 24, and 40% had 3 or more convictions.[22]

And one more *vital fact!*

- **Bullies can change.** The reality is *not* "once a bully, always a bully." For those willing to change, the Bible says, *"I will give you a new heart and put a new spirit in you; I will remove from you your heart of stone and give you a heart of flesh. And I will put my Spirit in you and move you to follow my decrees and be careful to keep my laws"* (Ezekiel 36:26–27).

God's Word speaks strongly to those who choose evil over good and who turn from truth and embrace lies ...

"You love evil rather than good, falsehood rather than speaking the truth."
(Psalm 52:3)

Popular girls began to feign romantic interest and make inappropriate sexual references toward Steve. Their boyfriends shoved Steve into lockers, knocked books out of his hands, and kneed him in the thighs to watch him collapse to the floor.

"This was great entertainment for them," Steve recalls. "It was a nightmare I thought would never end. I prayed for death. I never told anyone. I was too frightened—too ashamed."[23]

Steve was on the outside looking in, and those who enjoyed the security of their peer group forcefully kept him out. For newcomers and those who have been rejected, closed social systems are difficult to enter, yet still they seek acceptance. This creates an ideal environment for bullying. However, healthy social groups foster an atmosphere that discourages bullying by accepting new and old members alike, just as they are.

> "Do nothing out of selfish ambition
> or vain conceit. Rather, in humility
> value others above yourselves."
> (Philippians 2:3)

Social Cliques ...

▶ Are exclusive, closed systems that are difficult for new members to join

▶ Exist with strict requirements for members with strong pressure to conform

▶ Have one controlling personality at the top who calls the shots

▶ Consider those outside the group as being inferior in status and as targets of ridicule

Healthy Peer Groups ...

▶ Are inclusive, open systems that are eager for new members to join

▶ Exist with minimum requirements for members and little pressure to conform

▶ Have several personalities at the top who poll the members regarding their desires for the group

▶ Consider those outside the group to be equal to them in status and deserving of respect

Steve's bullies attempted to feel significant in sadistic ways. He suffered severe emotional and physical trauma as they continually cornered him in the locker room.

The "grand finale," however, was the most horrendous, the most humiliating bullying ritual inflicted on him. Referring to it as "The Golden Shower," multiple boys simultaneously urinate on Steve's unclothed, unprotected body. Devastated and demoralized, Steve curled up in a fetal position in a corner of the cold, hard shower and cried ... and cried ... bitter, gut-wrenching tears.[24]

Throughout all the bullying episodes Steve suffered in silence, shame paralyzing and preventing him from getting the help he so desperately needs.

How similar Steve's experience is to Psalm 17 ...

"They close up their callous hearts,
and their mouths speak with arrogance.
They have tracked me down,
they now surround me, with eyes alert,
to throw me to the ground."
(Psalm 17:10–11)

In truth, everyone has been created with three God-given inner needs: the needs for love, significance, and security.[25] Bullies seek to meet one or more of these needs through illegitimate means. If someone felt insignificant earlier in life, bullying is a way to feel significant now. Because they felt powerless in the past, they can put pressure on people and feel powerful, but it's an inappropriate sense of power. Instead, God wants to give us His power to live a godly life through belief in Jesus ...

"I pray that the eyes of your heart may be enlightened in order that you may know the hope to which he has called you, the riches of his glorious inheritance in his holy people, and his incomparably great power for us who believe." (Ephesians 1:18-19)

Know the Three God-Given Inner Needs

▶ **Love**—to know that someone is unconditionally committed to our best interest

"My command is this: Love each other as I have loved you" (John 15:12).

▶ **Significance**—to know that our lives have meaning and purpose

"I cry out to God Most High, to God who fulfills his purpose for me" (Psalm 57:2 ESV).

▶ **Security**—to feel accepted and a sense of belonging

"Whoever fears the LORD has a secure fortress, and for their children it will be a refuge" (Proverbs 14:26).

The Ultimate Need-Meeter

Whether a bully, victim, or bystander, all must realize that only God can meet our deepest inner needs. He gave us these inner needs so that we would come to know Him as our Need-Meeter.

Our needs are divinely designed to draw us into a deeper dependence on Christ. God did not create any person or position or any amount of power or possessions to meet the deepest needs in our lives. If a person or thing *could* meet all our needs, we wouldn't need God!

The Lord will use circumstances and bring positive people into our lives as an extension of His care and compassion, but ultimately only God can satisfy all the needs of our hearts.

The apostle Paul revealed this truth by first asking, *"What a wretched man I am. Who will rescue me from this body that is subject to death?"* He then answers his own question by saying he is saved by *"Jesus Christ our Lord!"* (Romans 7:24–25).

All along, the Lord planned to meet our deepest needs for ...

▶ **Love**

> *"I [the Lord] have loved you with an everlasting love; I have drawn you with unfailing kindness"* (Jeremiah 31:3).

▶ **Significance**

> *"'For I know the plans I have for you,' declares the LORD, 'plans to prosper you and not to*

harm you, plans to give you hope and a future'"
(Jeremiah 29:11).

▶ Security

"The LORD himself goes before you and will be with you; he will never leave you nor forsake you. Do not be afraid; do not be discouraged" (Deuteronomy 31:8).

The truth is that our God-given needs for love, significance, and security can be legitimately met in Christ Jesus! Philippians 4:19 makes it plain ...

"My God will meet all your needs according to the riches of his glory in Christ Jesus."

WHAT IS the Root Cause of Bullying?

Bullying is rooted in a wrong belief, aided and abetted by those who turn a blind eye and a deaf ear.

Young Steve Hunter finally summoned the courage to tell his gym teacher about the painful pulverizing, omitting no details. As powerful emotions began to overcome him, Steve started shaking uncontrollably and crying. The teacher's eyes—primarily fixated on the sports page of the newspaper before him—only momentarily darted to Steve's face.

But when all was said and done, Steve's bravely vulnerable disclosure was met with callous indifference. "Sorry. I can't do anything. You will just have to take it like a man. Go get dressed. You'll be late for class."[26]

Steve was first stunned with disbelief, then distracted in horror as he noticed a window looking into the locker room. There, with fierce faces and mocking mouths, were Steve's abusers, peering like predators about to pounce on their prey. Only a short time later, Steve was again subject to their locker-room cruelty and brutality ... and the infamous "Golden Shower."

Forced to endure their arrogant assaults yet again, he suffered alone, while his tormentors ...

" ... scoff, and speak with malice;
with arrogance they threaten oppression."
(Psalm 73:8)

Both the bully and the bullied believe lies that keep them trapped in a cycle of harmful behaviors. However, replacing lies with God's truth will lead to changed hearts and changed lives.

▶ WRONG BELIEF FOR THE BULLY

"If I push people around, they will respect me— then I'll feel important and significant."

RIGHT BELIEF OF THE BULLY

"I must treat others with respect in order to receive respect. I don't need to push others down to feel powerful. By giving Christ control of my life I'm relying on His power in me to fulfill me."

"His divine power has given us everything we need for a godly life through our knowledge of

him who called us by his own glory and goodness"
(2 Peter 1:3).

▶ Wrong Belief for the Bullied Victim

"I must deserve to be treated like this because I'm unlovable, insignificant, and insecure."

Right Belief of the Bullied Victim

"I can withstand the taunts of the bullies in my life because Christ lives inside me. He promises to meet my deepest needs and to give me strength. I may be distraught, but I'm not destroyed."

"We are hard pressed on every side, but not crushed; perplexed, but not in despair; persecuted, but not abandoned; struck down, but not destroyed" (2 Corinthians 4:8–9).

▶ Wrong Belief for the Bystander:

Apathetic Bystander: "This is not my fight, it's none of my business."

Passive Bystander: "If I try to stop this, I could also become a target."

Right Belief of the Bystander:

Protective Bystander: "I can't just stand here and do nothing. I must try to stop it. That is what Jesus would do—and that's what He would want me to do."

"He rescued me from my powerful enemy, from my foes, who were too strong for me" (Psalm 18:17).

Thankfully, the bullying came to an abrupt end in Steve's life when he moved from Victoria to Houston. Steve refers to this time as "the day of jubilee" because he was no longer victimized by others. He took up karate, built self-confidence, and eventually saw a blessing emerge from his traumatic experiences.

Today, Steve can truly say he has a "heart for those who can't stand up for themselves ... an empathy that moves you to act, to walk alongside." And Steve humbly and profoundly observes, "I'm the person I didn't have."[27] As a Licensed Professional Counselor with two earned doctoral degrees, he teaches counseling on the college level and has counseled many bullies as well as those who have been bullied—from personal experience. He encourages both to find healing through personal disclosure, sharing their experiences with others who need hope for their hearts. "With sharing experiences" Steve has learned "there's freedom."[28]

For indeed, Jesus said ...

> " ... the truth will set you free."
> (John 8:32)

True security is found in a relationship with God. Our hearts seek to be bonded with our Maker established through a personal relationship with Jesus Christ.

#1 God's Purpose for You is *Salvation*.

What was God's motivation in sending Jesus Christ to earth?

To express His love for you by saving you! The Bible says, *"God so loved the world that he gave his one and only Son, that whoever believes in him shall not perish but have eternal life. For God did not send his Son into the world to condemn the world, but to save the world through him"* (John 3:16–17).

What was Jesus' purpose in coming to earth?

To forgive your sins, to empower you to have victory over sin, and to enable you to live a fulfilled life! Jesus said, *"I have come that they may have life, and that they may have it more abundantly"* (John 10:10 NKJV).

#2 Your Problem is *Sin*.

What exactly is sin?

Sin is living independently of God's standard—knowing what is right, but choosing what is wrong. The Bible says, *"If anyone, then, knows the good they ought to do and doesn't do it, it is sin for them"* (James 4:17).

What is the major consequence of sin?

Spiritual death, eternal separation from God. Scripture states, *"Your iniquities [sins] have separated you from your God"* (Isaiah 59:2).

"The wages of sin is death, but the gift of God is eternal life in Christ Jesus our Lord" (Rom. 6:23).

God's Provision for You is the *Savior*.

Can anything remove the penalty for sin?

Yes! Jesus died on the cross to personally pay the penalty for your sins. The Bible says, *"God demonstrates his own love for us in this: While we were still sinners, Christ died for us"* (Romans 5:8).

What is the solution to being separated from God?

Belief in (entrusting your life to) Jesus Christ as the only way to God the Father. Jesus says, *"I am the way and the truth and the life. No one comes to the Father except through me"* (John 14:6). *"Believe in the Lord Jesus, and you will be saved"* (Acts 16:31).

#3 Your Part is *Surrender*.

Give Christ control of your life, entrusting yourself to Him.

"Jesus said to his disciples, 'Whoever wants to be my disciple, must deny themselves and take up their cross [die to their own self-rule] *and follow me. For whoever wants to save their life will lose it, but whoever loses their life for me will find it. What good will it be for someone to gain the whole world, yet forfeit their soul?'"* (Matthew 16:24–26).

Place your faith in (rely on) Jesus Christ as your personal Lord and Savior and reject your "good works" as a means of earning God's approval.

"It is by grace you have been saved, through faith—and this is not from yourselves, it is the gift of God—not by works, so that no one can boast" (Ephesians 2:8–9).

The moment you choose to receive Jesus as your Lord and Savior—entrusting your life to Him—His Spirit lives inside you. Then you have new power to live the fulfilled life God has planned for you.

If you want to be fully forgiven by God and become the person God created you to be, you can tell Him in a simple, heartfelt prayer like this:

PRAYER OF SALVATION

*"God, I want a real relationship with You.
I admit that many times I've chosen to go
my own way instead of Your way.
Please forgive me for my sins.
Jesus, thank You for dying on the cross to
pay the penalty for my sins.
Come into my life to be
my Lord and my Savior.
Change me from the inside out and make
me the person You created me to be.
In Your holy name I pray. Amen."*

WHAT CAN YOU NOW EXPECT?

If you sincerely prayed this prayer, look at what God says about you! *"If the Son sets you free, you will be free indeed"* (John 8:36).

STEPS TO SOLUTION

Imagine posters of monsters covering the walls, plastic models of Frankenstein, the Mummy, and Dracula welcoming all who walk in the room. Picture a young boy with all this monster paraphernalia—monster masks, comic books, and magazines scattered around his bedroom. Hear his high-pitched voice on a reel-to-reel recording, creating tales of mad scientists and their mutant creations. All his monsters endure tortuous lives. All are despised and rejected. He can acutely relate. People stare at him in horror—appalled at his appearance. And he's *weary* of answering the same old question from other children: "What's wrong with your tongue?"[29]

This was Frank's daily experience as a child. His tongue was always swollen—continually protruding from his mouth. His drooling was incessant, oozing a fluid that hardened and scabbed. Eating was always painful as he tried to chew and swallow without using his tongue.[30]

Little is known about cystic hygroma, a birth defect that plagued Frank throughout his childhood and youth, causing him to struggle with a disfigured, inoperative tongue along with other medical complications. Another characteristic common to cystic hygroma is a small, slight stature which, for Frank, generated even more vicious ridicule from others.

Most people who know Frank Peretti today would describe the acclaimed author as extraordinarily creative, competent, and confident, but the word *bullied* would never cross their minds. He is more often associated with his novels, read by millions worldwide—his New York Times best sellers, including *This Present Darkness* and *Piercing the Darkness*.

He explains, "No wonder I kept those guys [the monsters] around. Somewhere in my head, planted there repeatedly was the notion that I was one of them—ugly, rejected, picked on, and somehow less worthy of membership in the world of normal kids. Increasingly, through the eyes of others, I saw myself as a monster."[31]

There is One who can relate to all those who ever felt like Frank did—the One called the Suffering Servant—Jesus. The Bible says ...

"Just as there were many who were
appalled at him—
his appearance was so disfigured beyond
that of any human being and his form
marred beyond human likeness. ...
He was despised and rejected by mankind,
a man of suffering, and familiar with pain.
Like one from whom people
hide their faces he was despised,
and we held him in low esteem."
(Isaiah 52:14; 53:3)

Tragically, the effects of bullying can last a lifetime. Therefore, whether you are a *bully*, are *being bullied*, or just standing by *witnessing bullying*, God's Word addresses what you need to do.

Key Verses to Memorize

For the Bully:

"'God opposes the proud
but shows favor to the humble.'
Humble yourselves, therefore,
under God's mighty hand,
that he may lift you up in due time."
(1 Peter 5:5–6)

For the Bullied:

"Fear of man will prove to be a snare,
but whoever trusts in the Lord
is kept safe."
(Proverbs 29:25)

For the Bystander:

"Rescue those being led away to death;
hold back those staggering
toward slaughter.
If you say, 'But we knew nothing about this,'
does not he who weighs the heart
perceive it?
Does not he who guards your life know it?
Will he not repay everyone
according to what they have done?"
(Proverbs 24:11–12)

At home, Frank was deeply loved and thoroughly affirmed. He felt completely "normal" in such a nurturing environment. But then, as Frank solemnly shares, "I had to go to school."[32] If the teasing and taunting in elementary school was like a bad dream, then Frank's junior high school years were a nightmare—in 3-D!

It began in an area of school where kids are the most vulnerable—the dreaded locker room, replete with showers—a place where classmates peek, compare, and ultimately condemn. Frank was undersized and underdeveloped. He was also overwhelmed with fear, hoping he could slip in and out of the shower under the radar of the boy bullies.

Undeniably, Frank endured much pain before discovering God's purpose, priority, and plan for his life—especially involving these excruciating years. Clearly, God had a plan that Frank knew nothing about, for God says ...

> "'I know the plans I have for you,'
> declares the LORD,
> 'plans to prosper you and not to harm you,
> plans to give you hope and a future.'"
> (Jeremiah 29:11)

My Personalized Plan

▶ **Assess personal pain from my past.**

- I will determine if I have buried pain from being a victim of bullying.

- I will evaluate how pain from my past affects my present behavior.

- I will consider how my bullying others attempts to illegitimately meet my unmet needs.

- I will pray for God's direction in confronting those who have previously bullied me.

  "If your brother or sister sins, go and point out their fault, just between the two of you. If they listen to you, you have won them over" (Matthew 18:15).

▶ **Choose to obey God's commands.**

- I will be kind to the weak and oppressed.

- I will value those who are bullied because they are made in God's image.

- I will defend those who cannot defend themselves.

- I will give preferential honor to others.

  "Be devoted to one another in love. Honor one another above yourselves" (Romans 12:10).

▶ **Seek forgiveness and restoration.**

- I will confess the sins of bullying to God, asking Him to change my heart.

- I will ask forgiveness from those I've bullied.
- I will attempt to build a relationship with those whom I hurt.
- I will commit to living with a heart of reconciliation.

"If it is possible, as far as it depends on you, live at peace with everyone" (Romans 12:18).

AS THE ONE BULLIED, I WILL ...

▶ **Enlist help from God and others.**

- I will share troubling incidents with those who can be trusted to offer compassionate biblical counsel.
- I will avoid any tendencies to isolate based on my fear and shame.
- I will pray continually for God's intervention and resolution when I'm in a bullying situation.
- I will spend time reading and memorizing Scriptures that identify God as my personal Refuge, Deliverer, and Redeemer.

"Trust in him at all times, you people; pour out your hearts to him, for God is our refuge" (Psalm 62:8).

"The LORD is my rock, my fortress and my deliverer" (2 Samuel 22:2).

"Our Redeemer—the LORD Almighty is his name—is the Holy One of Israel" (Isaiah 47:4).

▶ **Grasp the immeasurable worth of every person.**

- I will recognize that God does not favor the strong over the weak.

- I will draw encouragement from a greater dependence on God.

- I will remember that God uniquely gifts every person and has a unique plan for my life.

- I will find peace and hope in the unconditional love of God.

  "But he [Jesus] said to me, 'My grace is sufficient for you, for my power is made perfect in weakness'" (2 Corinthians 12:9).

▶ **Examine the need for forgiveness.**

- I will discern if resentment and bitterness have taken root.

- I will meditate on Jesus' words and follow His example concerning forgiveness.

- I will pray for those who have bullied me and ask for God's healing in their lives.

- I will ask others for help with accountability in sustaining a forgiving heart.

  "Bear with each other and forgive one another if any of you has a grievance against someone. Forgive as the Lord forgave you" (Colossians 3:13).

▶ **Refuse to participate in bullying.**

- I will risk the scorn and assault of my peers to do what I know is right.

- I will come alongside of anyone I see being bullied.

- I will lean on God for courage, wisdom, and strength when confronted with any bullying situation.

- I will recognize I don't have to be controlled by a bully's anger or intimidation.

  "Those people are zealous to win you over, but for no good. What they want is to alienate you from us, so that you may have zeal for them" (Galatians 4:17).

▶ **Remember that one day I will have to give an account to God for my actions—or inaction.**

- I will treat others as I want to be treated.

- I will confess to God my fear of bullies and my past failure to defend the bullied.

- I will talk through any conflicted feelings I have about intervening on behalf of the bullied.

- I will understand that God intends for me to be His ambassador of hope and peace.

  "So I strive always to keep my conscience clear before God and man" (Acts 24:16).

▶ **Resolve to take action when I see someone being bullied.**

- I will remember that kindness and decency are more valuable than personal popularity.

- I will stand up and speak up.

- I will report any bullying I see to a trusted adult.

- I will believe that Christ's power in me can give me wisdom to bring calm and help me overcome a bully's control.

  "Fools give full vent to their rage, but the wise bring calm in the end" (Proverbs 29:11).

HOW TO Respond When a Child Reports Bullying

Frank hoped not to be noticed by his peers in the locker room, but first he heard chatter and then laughter directed his way. "Hey, get a load of this!" Within seconds a group of hecklers had closed in on him. Their cruel, stinging put-downs penetrated to the very core of his soul. "Ugly. Wimp. Gross. Little girl."[33]

Frank was bullied all three years of junior high and throughout his first year of high school until he finally spilled out every detail of his torturous ordeal in a letter to his gym teacher. Thanks to the compassion of school administrators, Frank was excused from P.E. class for the remainder of the year.[34]

Some people assume that bullied victims should "stick it out" and simply bear the brunt of the abuse, but the Bible says ...

> "In the paths of the wicked are snares and pitfalls, but those who would preserve their life stay far from them."
> (Proverbs 22:5)

Because of the astute actions of school administrators and their keen understanding of how to resolve bullying, Frank was forever freed from his teenage tormentors. With a new lease on life, Frank actually began to enjoy school, make friends, and heal, all the while developing a heart of compassion for the bullied—a compelling compassion that extended into adulthood.

After numerous surgeries, now Frank's tongue no longer protrudes from his mouth, and the famed Christian writer speaks out against the troubling social issue of bullying.

"I can see how God has worked through my wounds," Frank reflects.[35] Now a recovered victim of bullying, his empathy propels him to be a source for change in a world of intimidation.

His life vividly illustrates the truth of Scripture that God is a Redeemer ...

> "And we know that in all things God works for the good of those who love him, who have been called according to his purpose."
> (Romans 8:28)

If children tell you they are being bullied or if you merely suspect bullying, listen carefully. Take what they say seriously and show support by reinforcing that bullying is wrong. Assure every child: *There is no excuse for abuse*—it must stop. State that you will seek additional help to handle the problem. *Then do it!*

Dos and Don'ts

▶ **Don't** lose your patience.

Do listen carefully and ask questions to clarify the details.

▶ **Don't** overreact even if you feel anxious, upset, or angry.

Do remain calm, listen, and process the whole story.

▶ **Don't** blame the victim.

Do remember, the bully is the one at fault—the only one.

▶ **Don't** question bullied victims as if they've done something wrong or "deserve" to be bullied.

Do let children know you believe what they've said and you are willing to help.

▶ **Don't** charge in and take over like "gang busters."

Do stay rational and maintain control.

▶ **Don't** minimize the situation or underreact, especially if there is any mention of suicide.

Do seek professional help *immediately* with any hint or suspicion of suicide.

▶ **Don't** keep children in the dark about the reality of bullying.

Do strategize with each child. For example,

- Teach them not to react out of fear, which only fuels the fire of a bully.
- Ask if they have any ideas for changing the situation.
- Encourage them to say, "Stop it" or "Not funny" or "Cut it out," then walk away.
- Explain that ignoring the bully is one effective response—not engaging the bully helps defuse the situation.
- Advise them to stay with a buddy or friend—there is strength in numbers.
- Instruct them to *always* talk with a safe adult whenever bullying occurs.

Let victims know what God says about this troubling situation. The Bible says ...

"God is just: He will pay back trouble to those who trouble you ... "
(2 Thessalonians 1:6)

QUESTION: "One of my daughter's friends posted a mean message about another girl. My daughter says it's only a joke, but I'm concerned, what should I do?"

ANSWER: Don't assume the incident is not a "big deal." Explain to your daughter when she uses e-mail, texts, or social media to intentionally intimidate, shame, or hurt others, it is *cyberbullying,* and cyberbullying is abusive and unacceptable.

How to protect children against cyberbullying:

▶ **Monitor** your child's online habits. Use parental controls, filtering software, and online tracking programs. The Bible says, *"Wisdom will save you from evil people* [bullies], *from those whose words are twisted"* (Proverbs 2:12 NLT).

▶ **Report** instances of cyberbullying to the appropriate authorities. This might include: parents, teachers or administrators, church workers, and, in serious cases when warranted, law enforcement authorities.

- Most online service providers have a policy against using their service to bully. Review your provider's "Terms of Service" agreement and explain it to your child in simple terms. If the terms were violated, report the violation to the service provider.

- If your child is bullied online, give instructions not to open e-mails or messages from the bully (who might have a read receipt requested to monitor the effect of the bullying).

- If your child is caught being a cyberbully, restrict access to all electronic tools. Let the child know that online access is a privilege, not a right.

▶ **Become involved** in your child's online community. Monitor their use of computers, cellphones, tablets, and online activity to make sure it is used responsibly.

Though a cyberbully may hide behind a computer screen, God sees the wrong deeds done in secret and knows the wrong motives in each person's heart.

> "There is no deep shadow, no utter darkness, where evildoers can hide."
> (Job 34:22)

Self-Defense

QUESTION: **"My 10-year-old son has been bullied since he started school this year, and now he wants to take judo. I don't want him to retaliate, but I want him to feel safe. Is it wrong for him to be able to defend himself this way?"**

ANSWER: While the cry of a bullied child's heart should be, *"Keep me safe, LORD, from the hands of the wicked; protect me from the violent, who devise ways to trip my feet"* (Psalm 140:4), this does not preclude employing self-defense when it is warranted.

Taking a self-defense class may help your son gain confidence to defend himself when he's accosted by a bully. Since he has expressed interest, speak with him about the reasons he wants to take judo and discern whether his motivation is to *protect* himself or to *punish* his bully.

A judo class could develop several positive traits and encourage your son to ...

▶ Exhibit confidence and self-assurance

▶ Employ body language that exudes confidence like a shield

▶ Be better prepared to defend himself and escape to safety

▶ Feel a sense of independence and pride

Teach and model the wisdom of Proverbs 22:3 ...

"The prudent see danger and take refuge,
but the simple keep going
and pay the penalty."

"That's just the way things are."[36] Regarding bullying, this saying seems to be the mind-set among too many school administrators and teachers, according to Frank Peretti.

Rather than intervening, they tolerate a "survival of the fittest" environment where weaker children are left to fend for themselves. "There's the idea that somehow manliness is equated with cruelty; if you're cruel, if you're tough, if you one-up everybody physically, that makes you a man," Frank has observed. "That's the way it was in gym class anyway. The teacher's demeanor just permeated the rest of the class."[37]

In truth, those who are continually abused live with a crushed spirit and do not thrive well at school or anywhere. Proverbs 15:4 says ...

> "The soothing tongue is a tree of life,
> but a perverse tongue crushes the spirit."

This is why schools must help stop bullying by practicing three vital *R*s:

▶ **Rules**: Students must know that teachers are in charge and that hurting other students will not be tolerated. Set and enforce rules regarding bullying.

▶ **Rights**: Every student has the right to not be hurt and to learn in a safe environment.

▶ **Responsibility**: All adults at school–including administrators, teachers, aides, and cafeteria staff must be responsible for supervision. One of the best ways to stop bullying is to take away the audience. The most effective deterrent to bullying is when students are taught to be courageous enough to report it and not to take part when they see it occur.

Schools can help stop bullying by taking these three steps:

1 Educate the students.

▶ Define bullying by learning the difference between normal conflict and bullying.

▶ Differentiate the roles between the bullies, the targets, and the bystanders.

▶ Distinguish the vital role of courageous bystanders.

"The teaching of the wise is a fountain of life, turning a person from the snares of death" (Proverbs 13:14)

2 Enlist the faculty.

▶ Take action: Don't ignore bullying behavior.

- Sign a faculty anti-bullying pledge: "We the faculty agree to join together to stamp out bullying."
- Create or adopt a Bully-Blocking curriculum as well as a support system for bullied students.

- Develop a clear school policy on bullying with specific repercussions.
- Display the policy in all classrooms and around the school.

▷ Train the faculty to handle all bullying incidents.

- Discuss proactive bully-blocking measures (like eating lunch with a new or excluded student).
- Formulate a reporting system to inform and educate parents when bullying occurs.
- Report all bullying to the principal.
- Offer counseling to bullies, bystanders, and bullied students.

▷ Ensure a safe atmosphere where students who report bullying are confident that the bullying will be quickly addressed and stopped, not ignored.

- Display the rules and repercussions against bullying.
- Reinforce the repercussions every time bullying occurs
- Teach worth of all and respect for all.
- Teach empathy for others.

"Learn to do right; seek justice. Defend the oppressed" (Isaiah 1:17).

3 Engage the students in preparing class pledges.

▶ **The Bully-Blockers Club**

- We will never bully anyone.
- We will treat everyone with kindness and respect.
- We will include those who are being left out.
- We will help students who are being bullied.
- We will report any bullying we know about.
- Signed _____

"Do not let any unwholesome talk come out of your mouths, but only what is helpful for building others up according to their needs, that it may benefit those who listen" (Ephesians 4:29).

Telling vs. Tattling

QUESTION: "I know it's wrong to be a bully, but isn't it also wrong to be a tattletale?

ANSWER: One of the major obstacles in reporting bullying is the fear of being labeled a *tattletale*. However this is false fear because at the root, *tattling* is attempting to get someone *into trouble*, whereas *reporting* is attempting to get someone *out of trouble*.

"'Because the poor are plundered and the needy groan, I will now arise,' says the Lord. 'I will protect them from those who malign them.'"
(Psalm 12:5)

HOW TO Hold Kids Accountable for Bullying

During Frank's turbulent years, people rarely held kids accountable for bullying. Teachers insisted he press on in precarious environments, as did his parents, compounding his pain and further inciting his tormentors. Frank regretfully recalls, "No one, not one adult anywhere, said, 'You know what, Frank? What's happening to you is wrong. You shouldn't be putting up with that.'"[38]

Bullies need to be confronted, challenged, and shown how to change by someone in authority, as Scripture directs ...

" ... remember this: Whoever turns a sinner
from the error of their way
will save them from death
and cover over a multitude of sins."
(James 5:20)

As you make efforts to hold others accountable for their hurtful actions ...

▶ **Take warning signs of bullying seriously.** Don't rationalize, "Kids will be kids. It's just a phase. They'll grow out of it." If there are escalating symptoms, devote focused attention to the problem before it gets worse.

The biblical book of wisdom says, *"The prudent see danger and take refuge, but the simple keep going and pay the penalty"* (Proverbs 27:12).

▶ **Plan what you are going to say** to the bullying child and the parents, then enforce repercussions.[39]

"For these are rebellious people, deceitful children, children unwilling to listen to the LORD's instruction" (Isaiah 30:9).

▶ **Make the heart of the bullying child** your highest priority by making a plan of redemption. You can't dictate the condition of a child's heart, but if there is sincere remorse with a repentant heart, a plan of redemption can include offering restitution to those who have been bullied.[40]

"Now it is required that those who have been given a trust must prove faithful" (1 Corinthians 4:2).

▶ **Tailor your actions** and repercussions to the child's age.

- **Kindergarten and younger children** likely do not understand how devastating bullying can be. Share what the Bible says about treating others with kindness and respect: *"Be kind and compassionate to one another, forgiving each other, just as in Christ God forgave you"* (Ephesians 4:32).

- **Elementary-age children** understand that bullying is wrong, but they might not truly grasp how it makes others feel. Teach children God's displeasure when *"their hearts plot violence, and their lips talk about making trouble"* (Proverbs 24:2).

- **Upper elementary-age children** know bullying is wrong and why it is wrong. Remind them that *"Whoever sows injustice reaps calamity, and the rod they wield in fury will be broken"* (Proverbs 22:8).

- **Teenagers** are well aware of the pain bullying can inflict and can find exceptionally sophisticated—and clandestine—ways to perpetrate their acts. Share encouragement from Proverbs 13:18 with your teen: *"Whoever disregards discipline comes to poverty and shame, but whoever heeds correction is honored."*

HOW PARENTS Can Prevent Bullying

Parents send children off to school and then, from the sidelines, guide them through the challenging changes of a new and complicated environment. Although not present every minute of every day, parents can prevent bullying from taking root by preparing and empowering children to confront and conquer bullying.

Seven Biblical Steps to Prevent Bullying

1 **Explain** how God makes everyone unique and valuable.

- "God designed people to be different and unique from each other."

- "Accept and value your unique traits because each person is a masterpiece of God's creativity."
- "God also designed people to be connected with one another—to help one another."

"As iron sharpens iron, so one person sharpens another" (Proverbs 27:17).

2 **Model relationships** of respect, kindness, civility, and self-control.

- Children most often learn how to interact and relate to others by observing and interacting with their parents, siblings, and other family and friends.
- Critically evaluate how you communicate and relate with your spouse and other family members.
- Reflect on your response when dealing with people who annoy, disappoint, or frustrate you.

"In everything set them an example by doing what is good. In your teaching show integrity, seriousness and soundness of speech that cannot be condemned" (Titus 2:7–8).

3 **Purposefully connect** with your child's online community.

- Develop age-appropriate guidelines with your child concerning blogging and social media services, including the subject matter, tone, and time devoted to the Internet.

- Join and be active or at least monitor your child's connections and communication on message boards, blogs, school-sponsored sites, or other social media.
- Review the "Terms of Use and Community Standards" of social media platforms to ensure compliance and follow designated procedures to report violations.

"Whoever would love life and see good days must keep their tongue from evil and their lips from deceitful speech. They must turn from evil and do good; they must seek peace and pursue it. For the eyes of the Lord are on the righteous and his ears are attentive to their prayer, but the face of the Lord is against those who do evil" (1 Peter 3:10–12).

4 **Own responsibility** for preventing and stopping bullying.

- Bullying is not someone else's problem to resolve—it is our shared obligation.
- Emphasize to your children their responsibility to stand up for themselves and for others.
- Children and teens are not equipped to handle harassment and abuse alone but need a support network of parents, educators, and peers.

"For the sins of their mouths, for the words of their lips, let them be caught in their pride" (Psalm 59:12).

5 **Work** with your community to prevent bullying and protect children.

- Engage with parents, community leaders, teachers, and school officials to prevent and end bullying.

- Draft and present a contract that:

  ▶ Defines and prohibits bullying

  ▶ Outlines a clear, safe structure for reporting bullying

  ▶ Stipulates the consequences for engaging in bullying

  ▶ Involves parents, students, and educators

  ▶ Requires clear communication to the community

- If you find your child is involved in bullying, enlist the assistance of a counselor or an objective, trustworthy, and wise third party.

"Plans fail for lack of counsel, but with many advisers they succeed" (Proverbs 15:22).

6 **Encourage** your children to stand up for themselves and others.

- Train your children to take responsibility for their own feelings, thoughts, and actions—learning to be grateful for their own unique qualities without comparing themselves to others.

- Clarify that each one of us should carry our own load and take responsibility for ourselves, but bullying is a heavy burden that requires the involvement and assistance of others to resolve.

- Explain that disengaging or ignoring bullying indicates they (as bystanders) are simply giving tacit approval to the abuse; however, many bullying situations can be stopped if they learn how to intervene.[41]

"Carry each other's burdens, and in this way you will fulfill the law of Christ. If anyone thinks they are something when they are not, they deceive themselves. Each one should test their own actions. Then they can take pride in themselves alone, without comparing themselves to someone else, for each one should carry their own load" (Galatians 6:2–5).

7 **Redeem** the heart of your bullying child or reclaim the dignity of your bullied child.

- Explore the hidden motivations that have contributed to bullying by determining whether the bully feels loved, valued, and accepted or if the aggressor has been bullied in the past.

- Agree in writing with each involved student and parent concerning safeguards, requirements, and penalties to end the bullying.

- Help your bullied child manage the process of healing and forgiveness.

"Do to others as you would have them do to you" (Luke 6:31).

▶ **Find someone you trust.** Go to an authority figure (parent, administrator, teacher, coach, or counselor) as well as someone in your peer group to talk about the bullying. Gaining insights from different perspectives can help you make wise choices.

▶ **Be completely honest about your experiences and feelings.** Present an accurate picture of what has been happening and don't hold back.

▶ **Learn to say, "No."** Building strong and healthy boundaries demonstrates self-respect and encourages others to respect you as well.

▶ **Ask about what kinds of social skills or techniques might help overcome or prevent bullying.** Preventing isolation, developing friendships that offer mutual protection, or using humor to diffuse difficult situations are all valuable abilities that require practice.

▶ **Remain calm.** Do not demonstrate any extreme reactions. Cowering in fear, angry retaliation, or tearful escape may only encourage a bully by giving them a false feeling of power and control over you.

▶ **Finally, never give up!** If you look for help but don't find it, keep looking. Tell your story to others until you find the help that you need. Don't give in to bullies but practice being assertive and standing your ground.

If you are being bullied, find help from Hope For The Heart by calling us at 1-800-488-HOPE (4673).

HOW TO Practice Intervening—The Bystander

His name is John, and Frank Peretti also calls him *unforgettable*. Another typical scenario unfolded with a bully, someone Frank describes as a "character with a truckload of dysfunction."[42] All of a sudden, John intervened and when he stepped up, the bully backed down. With a commanding presence and a calm voice, John convinced the bully that there were better ways to spend his time, so the bully went away—for good. Never again did he try to threaten or intimidate.

Decades later, whenever he remembers that moment, Frank still thanks God for John, forever grateful for a bystander who became *the difference maker*. "He came between me and harm. He stood on that wall. I think he's the only one who ever did."[43]

John models the call of Scripture ...

"Speak up and judge fairly; defend the
rights of the poor and needy"
(Proverbs 31:9).

The vast majority of people are not actively involved in the insidious intimidation of bullying, but by choosing to become the "silent majority," over time, they become increasingly desensitized with a diminished empathy for victims.

Some bystanders become excited or even mesmerized by violence and choose to watch it like a video game instead of getting involved. Bystanders are the most underused resource in bullying. Yet, changing how bystanders respond to bullying is essential to achieving a solution.

▶ **Empower** bystanders to quickly become engaged in the drama playing out in front of them, by using the "role play" technique—you take the role of a bully and have the bystanders confront with phrases like these:

- "Stop It! Stop hitting him! That's wrong!"
- "You shouldn't make fun of her! Stop treating her that way!"
- "Leave them alone! If you don't stop, I'm going to tell (name of authority) right now!" or "I'm going to call 911 right now!"
- "Did you just do that? Why did you do that?" During the role play, practice following through on what they say, knowing that *what they say, they will do.*

"Speak up for those who cannot speak for themselves, for the rights of all who are destitute" (Proverbs 31:8).

▶ **Encourage** bystanders to take a stand for the one targeted.

- Stop rumors—Don't pass on hurtful notes, messages, or gossip.
- Don't laugh or even smile at put-downs or mean jokes.
- Say "Hi" to new students or someone who just needs a friend.
- Publicly praise the bystander's kindness and courage toward the victim.

"Turn from evil and do good; seek peace and pursue it" (Psalm 34:14).

▶ **Become** a conduit for change.

- Encourage outsiders to join activities.
- Give support to those who is being picked on.
- Let authorities know when someone needs help.
- Become a peer mediator at school.

"If anyone has material possessions and sees a brother or sister in need but has no pity on them, how can the love of God be in that person? Dear children, let us not love with words or speech but with actions and in truth" (1 John 3:17–18).

▶ **Take** a stand on four levels.

- LEVEL 1: Withhold support from the bully by not participating (for example, not watching, laughing, or gossiping).
- LEVEL 2: Support the victim in front of the bully.
- LEVEL 3: Confront the bully in front of others.
- LEVEL 4: Join forces to protect the victim.

"Call the evildoer to account for his wickedness that would not otherwise be found out" (Psalm 10:15).

The cycle of verbal, emotional, and physical violence must be stopped. Since the code of silence is a bully's greatest source of protection, courageous bystanders must stand up for what is right.

"Bring to an end the violence of the wicked
and make the righteous secure—
you, the righteous God
who probes minds and hearts."
(Psalm 7:9)

Words! They can lavish love—and they can lacerate lives. They can compassionately comfort and they can cruelly condemn. Frank is well aware that careful instruction concerning words is necessary to heal the wounds of bullying. "Having been hurt by words, I have a better appreciation for what words can do. Wanting to be like Jesus, I try to watch my mouth; rather than lacing my conversation with sarcasm—an arrow with the tip only slightly dulled—I attempt to speak words of encouragement, and I try to uplift people I meet."[44]

After multiple bouts of bullying, many victims lose hope and some lose their will to live. That is why words of hope—hope for change—is essential.

> "Hope deferred makes the heart sick,
> but a longing fulfilled is a tree of life."
> (Proverbs 13:12)

Adults can start a conversation with a child bully in a simple, straightforward way, like this:

▶ "There's an old saying that goes something like this: *Treat other people in the same way you want them to treat you.*"

▶ Then ask ...

- "Have you ever heard these words before?" "What do you think it means?"

- "Is that what you would want from others?"

▶ "Think back to the first time you were belittled, harassed, or bullied."

- "How did that make you feel?"
- "How old were you? What happened?"

▶ "Did you know ... ?"

- Bullying eventually backfires; it makes everyone miserable—even bullies.
- People do feel intimidated by bullies, but people don't respect bullies.

▶ "Do you want people to respect you?"

- To applaud your strength or be appalled at your strength being used to hurt the weak?
- To value you for using your power to pull someone up or vilify you for using your power to push someone down?

▶ "Do you want others to admire you?"

- To think highly of you for protecting others or to think badly of you for picking on others?
- To admire you for helping others or to disrespect you for hurting others?

People everywhere are looking for heroes—people they can respect, even admire. Instead of being a negative influence by hurting people, you can be the hero who helps people, the one who has a positive influence on others. You can be respected by both the weak and the strong.

To the power seekers, Jesus said ...

"Those who exalt themselves
will be humbled, and those who humble
themselves will be exalted."
(Matthew 23:12)

Now that puts real power into perspective!

The bully seeks power to
"lord it over" others.
But the only true Lord wisely said,
*"Do to others what you would have them
do to you"* (Matthew 7:12).
Why not do it His way? After all,
He changed the world!

—June Hunt

SCRIPTURES TO MEMORIZE

What hope do I have when being bullied leaves me feeling **hard pressed, persecuted, perplexed,** and **struck down?**

*"We are **hard pressed** on every side, but not crushed; **perplexed,** but not in despair; **persecuted,** but not abandoned; **struck down,** but not destroyed."* (2 Corinthians 4:8–9)

How **can I do all things—who strengthens me?**

*"**I can do all things** through Christ **who strengthens me.**"* (Philippians 4:13 NKJV)

Are the attacks against me **hidden from God's sight** or **must** my attacker someday **give account?**

*"Nothing in all creation is **hidden from God's sight.** Everything is uncovered and laid bare before the eyes of him to whom we **must give account.**"* (Hebrews 4:13)

What may happen if you **make friends with a hot-tempered person** or **one easily angered?**

*"Do not **make friends with a hot-tempered person,** do not associate with **one easily angered,** or you may learn their ways and get yourself ensnared."* (Proverbs 22:24–25)

Is it a **sin** if a bystander **knows to do good** and help, but **doesn't do it?**

*"If anyone, then, **knows** the **good** they ought **to do** and **doesn't do it, it is sin** for them."* (James 4:17)

NOTES

1. Jill Smolowe, "Bullied to Death?" *People*, April 26, 2010.

2. Smolowe, "Bullied to Death?"

3. Smolowe, "Bullied to Death?"

4. Tonja R. Nansel, Mary Overpeck, Ramani S. Pilla, W. June Ruan, Bruce Simons-Morton, Peter Scheidt "Bullying Behaviors Among US Youth" *Journal of the American Medical Association*, vol. 285, no. 16 (Chicago: American Medical Association, 2001), 2096.

5. Ellie Young, America Boye, David Nelson, "Relational Aggression: Understanding, Identifying, and Responding in Schools" *Psychology in the Schools*, vol. 43, no. 3, 297.

6. Smolowe, "Bullied to Death?"

7. Liz McNeil, "Suicide in South Hadley Bullied to Death?" *People*, February 22, 2010.

8. Olweus Bullying Prevention Program, "Why Shouldn't We Use a Conflict Resolution or Peer Mediation Program to Address Bullying Issues?" http://www.violencepreventionworks.org/public/faqs.page.

9. Smolowe, "Bullied to Death?"

10. Sarah Anne Hughes, "Phoebe Prince Suicide: What Can Be Done About Bullying" *The Washington Post: WorldViews*, May 5, 2011, http://www.washingtonpost.com/blogs/blogpost/post/phoebe-prince-suicide-what-can-be-done-about-bullying/2011/05/05/AFpd6VyF_blog.html.

11. Smolowe, "Bullied to Death?"

12. Nancy Gibbs, "When Bullying Goes Criminal," *Time*, April 19, 2010.

13. Dan Olweus, "Peer Harassment: A critical Analysis and Some Important Issues," *Peer Harassment in School*, ed. J. Juvonen and S. Graham (New York: Guilford Publications, 2001), 3–20.

14. Hughes, "Phoebe Prince Suicide: What Can Be Done About Bullying" *The Washington Post: WorldViews*, May 5, 2011, http://www.washingtonpost.com/blogs/blogpost/

post/phoebe-prince-suicide-what-can-be-done-about-bullying/2011/05/05/AFpd6VyF_blog.html.

15. For all elements of Lynzee's story, Lynzee Benoit, unpublished personal communication with the author March 2014.

16. Committee for Children, "Steps to Respect Program Guide: Research Review" (Seattle: Committee for Children, 2005), 19–20, http://www.cfchildren.org/Portals/0/STR/STR_DOC/Research_Review_STR.pdf.

17. Debbie Pincus, "Child and Teen Bullying: How to Help When Your Kid Is Bullied" *Empowering Parents* (n.p.: Legacy Publishing, April 2012), http://www.empoweringparents.com/article_print.php?id=296.

18. Steve Hunter, *Make-Believers: Ending the Pretending to Live Happily Ever After* (Garland, TX: Hannibal Books, 2006), 31.

19. Committee for Children, "Steps to Respect Program Guide: Research Review"

20. Rachel Simmons, "The Nine Most Common Myths About Bullying" *Newsweek*, October 15, 2010.

21. Nansel, Overpeck, Pilla, Ruan, Simons-Morton, Scheidt "Bullying Behaviors Among US Youth" *Journal of the American Medical Association*, vol. 285, no. 16, http://jama.jamanetwork.com/article.aspx?articleid=193774.

22. James Fox, Delbert Elliott, R. Gil Kerlikowske, Sanford Newman, William Christeson, "Bullying Prevention Is Crime Prevention" (Washington, D.C.: Fight Crime: Invest in Kids, 2003), 2.

23. Hunter, *Make-Believers*, 36.

24. Hunter, *Make-Believers*, 35.

25. Lawrence J. Crabb, Jr., *Understanding People: Deep Longings for Relationship*, Ministry Resources Library (Grand Rapids: Zondervan, 1987), 15–16; Robert S. McGee, *The Search for Significance*, 2nd ed. (Houston, TX: Rapha, 1990), 27–30.

26. Hunter, *Make-Believers*, 34.

27. Steve Hunter, unpublished personal communication with the author, October 2012.

28. Steve Hunter, unpublished personal communication with the author, October 2012.

29. Frank Peretti, *No More Victims* (Nashville: Thomas Nelson, 2001), 23.

30. Frank Peretti, *No More Bullies* (Nashville: Thomas Nelson 2003), 36.

31. Peretti, *No More Victims*, 23.

32. Peretti, *No More Bullies*, 44.

33. Peretti, *No More Bullies*, 4.

34. Peretti, *No More Victims*, 46.

35. Frank Peretti, *The Wounded Spirit* (Nashville: Thomas Nelson, 2000), 183.

36. Tom Neven, "Book Review: *The Wounded Spirit*" (Colorado Springs, CO: Focus on the Family, 2001), http://www.families.org.au/default.aspx?go=article&aid=1270&tid=1.

37. Neven, "Book Review: *The Wounded Spirit*," http://www.families.org.au/default.aspx?go=article&aid=1270&tid=1.

38. Neven, "Book Review: *The Wounded Spirit*"

39. June Hunt with Jody Capehart, *Bonding with Your Teen through Boundaries*, revised edition (Wheaton: Crossway, 2010), 121.

40. Hunt with Capehart, *Bonding with Your Teen*, 122.

41. National Bullying Prevention Center, "Bullying Prevention Advocates Call for Social Movement to Address Effects of Bullying" (Minneapolis/St. Paul: PACER Center, October 6, 2011), http://www.pacer.org/bulying/about/pressrelease.asp?file=2011/nr20111006-2.asp.

42. Peretti, *No More Bullies*, 152.

43. Peretti, *No More Bullies*, 153.

44. Peretti, *The Wounded Spirit*, 183.

June Hunt's HOPE FOR THE HEART minibooks are biblically-based, and full of practical advice that is relevant, spiritually-fulfilling and wholesome.

HOPE FOR THE HEART TITLES

www.aspirepress.com